Chocolate _or_ Vanilla?

Quick Quizzes for BFFs

Thanks to my daughter, Brittany, and her best friend
Dominique, for all their insight and great ideas!

–L.M.

ISBN-13: 978-0-545-15602-8

ISBN-10: 0-545-15602-5

12 11 10 9 8 7 6 5 4   11 12 13 14/0

Printed in the U.S.A.   40

First printing, September 2009

Book design by Janet Kusmierski

Chocolate or Vanilla?

Quick Quizzes for BFFs

BY LIZZIE MACK

SCHOLASTIC INC.

New York   Toronto   London   Auckland   Sydney

Mexico City   New Delhi   Hong Kong   Buenos Aires

Hot or cold?

Milk and cookies or chips and salsa?

Sweet or tart?

Do you choose friends who are just like you,
or friends who have different tastes?

Take these quizzes, and then give them
to your friends.

How do they compare to you?

Quizzes are a fun way to learn
about the people you hang out with.

Enjoy!

TASTY TREATS
Everybody's gotta eat!

1. ⭘ Cake or ⭘ Ice cream?

2. Favorite dessert of all time?_____

3. ⭘ Chocolate ⭘ Vanilla or ⭘ Both?

4. ⭘ Potato chips or ⭘ Popcorn?

5. ⭘ Bring your lunch or ⭘ Eat cafeteria food?

6. ⭘ Waffles or ⭘ Pancakes?

7. ⭘ Muffins or ⭘ Cinnamon rolls?

8. Do you ⭘ Sit down for breakfast or

   ⭘ Grab something and run out the door?

9. ⭘ Eat out or ⭘ Take out?

10. ⭘ Fast food or ⭘ Fancy restaurant?

11. ⭘ Pizza or ⭘ Mac and cheese?

12. ⭘ Baked from scratch or ⭘ Bought from a bakery?

13. ⭘ Milkshake or ⭘ Smoothie?

14. ⭘ Wings or ⭘ Nachos?

15. Would you rather eat

    ⭘ 50 lbs of french fries or ⭘ 50 lbs of potato chips?

16. ◯ Chocolate milk ◯ Strawberry milk or ◯ Plain milk?

17. ◯ Hamburger or ◯ Hot dog?

18. ◯ Ketchup or ◯ Mustard?

19. ◯ Chunky peanut butter or ◯ Creamy peanut butter?

20. Favorite cake? _____

21. Would you rather eat ◯ Cookie dough or ◯ Baked cookies?

22. ◯ Sweet or ◯ Tart?

23. Buffalo wings: ◯ Mild or ◯ Hot and spicy?

24. ◯ Energy drinks or ◯ Soda?

25. Favorite food of all time? _____

WARNING ~ Gross questions ahead!

26. Would you rather eat ◯ Chocolate-covered ants or

    ◯ Chocolate-covered worms?

27. ◯ Roasted roaches or

    ◯ Mashed-up maggots?

    CW

28. ◯ Slime or ◯ Boogers?

29. ◯ Spaghetti with eyeballs or ◯ Macaroni and guts?

30. Would you rather drink ◯ A rotten banana milkshake or

    ◯ A sour strawberry smoothie?

TASTY TREATS
Everybody's gotta eat!

1. ◯ Cake or ◯ Ice cream?

2. Favorite dessert of all time?_____

3. ◯ Chocolate ◯ Vanilla or ◯ Both?

4. ◯ Potato chips or ◯ Popcorn?

5. ◯ Bring your lunch or ◯ Eat cafeteria food?

6. ◯ Waffles or ◯ Pancakes?

7. ◯ Muffins or ◯ Cinnamon rolls?

8. Do you ◯ Sit down for breakfast or

   ◯ Grab something and run out the door?

9. ◯ Eat out or ◯ Take out?

10. ◯ Fast food or ◯ Fancy restaurant?

11. ◯ Pizza or ◯ Mac and cheese?

12. ◯ Baked from scratch or ◯ Bought from a bakery?

13. ◯ Milkshake or ◯ Smoothie?

14. ◯ Wings or ◯ Nachos?

15. Would you rather eat

    ◯ 50 lbs of french fries or ◯ 50 lbs of potato chips?

16. ⊘ Chocolate milk ⊘ Strawberry milk or ⊘ Plain milk?

17. ⊘ Hamburger or ⊘ Hot dog?

18. ⊘ Ketchup or ⊘ Mustard?

19. ⊘ Chunky peanut butter or ⊘ Creamy peanut butter?

20. Favorite cake? _____

21. Would you rather eat ⊘ Cookie dough or ⊘ Baked cookies?

22. ⊘ Sweet or ⊘ Tart?

23. Buffalo wings: ⊘ Mild or ⊘ Hot and spicy?

24. ⊘ Energy drinks or ⊘ Soda?

25. Favorite food of all time? _____

WARNING ~ Gross questions ahead!

26. Would you rather eat ⊘ Chocolate-covered ants or

    ⊘ Chocolate-covered worms?

27. ⊘ Roasted roaches or

    ⊘ Mashed-up maggots?

28. ⊘ Slime or ⊘ Boogers?

29. ⊘ Spaghetti with eyeballs or ⊘ Macaroni and guts?

30. Would you rather drink ⊘ A rotten banana milkshake or

    ⊘ A sour strawberry smoothie?

TASTY TREATS
Everybody's gotta eat!

1. ○ Cake or ○ Ice cream?

2. Favorite dessert of all time?_____

3. ○ Chocolate ○ Vanilla or ○ Both?

4. ○ Potato chips or ○ Popcorn?

5. ○ Bring your lunch or ○ Eat cafeteria food?

6. ○ Waffles or ○ Pancakes?

7. ○ Muffins or ○ Cinnamon rolls?

8. Do you ○ Sit down for breakfast or

   ○ Grab something and run out the door?

9. ○ Eat out or ○ Take out?

10. ○ Fast food or ○ Fancy restaurant?

11. ○ Pizza or ○ Mac and cheese?

12. ○ Baked from scratch or ○ Bought from a bakery?

13. ○ Milkshake or ○ Smoothie?

14. ○ Wings or ○ Nachos?

15. Would you rather eat

    ○ 50 lbs of french fries or ○ 50 lbs of potato chips?

16. ◯ Chocolate milk ◯ Strawberry milk or ◯ Plain milk?

17. ◯ Hamburger or ◯ Hot dog?

18. ◯ Ketchup or ◯ Mustard?

19. ◯ Chunky peanut butter or ◯ Creamy peanut butter?

20. Favorite cake? _____

21. Would you rather eat ◯ Cookie dough or ◯ Baked cookies?

22. ◯ Sweet or ◯ Tart?

23. Buffalo wings: ◯ Mild or ◯ Hot and spicy?

24. ◯ Energy drinks or ◯ Soda?

25. Favorite food of all time? _____

WARNING ~ Gross questions ahead!

26. Would you rather eat ◯ Chocolate-covered ants or

    ◯ Chocolate-covered worms?

27. ◯ Roasted roaches or

    ◯ Mashed-up maggots?

28. ◯ Slime or ◯ Boogers?

29. ◯ Spaghetti with eyeballs or ◯ Macaroni and guts?

30. Would you rather drink ◯ A rotten banana milkshake or

    ◯ A sour strawberry smoothie?

TASTY TREATS

Everybody's gotta eat!

1. ◯ Cake or ◯ Ice cream?

2. Favorite dessert of all time?_____

3. ◯ Chocolate ◯ Vanilla or ◯ Both?

4. ◯ Potato chips or ◯ Popcorn?

5. ◯ Bring your lunch or ◯ Eat cafeteria food?

6. ◯ Waffles or ◯ Pancakes?

7. ◯ Muffins or ◯ Cinnamon rolls?

8. Do you ◯ Sit down for breakfast or

    ◯ Grab something and run out the door?

9. ◯ Eat out or ◯ Take out?

10. ◯ Fast food or ◯ Fancy restaurant?

11. ◯ Pizza or ◯ Mac and cheese?

12. ◯ Baked from scratch or ◯ Bought from a bakery?

13. ◯ Milkshake or ◯ Smoothie?

14. ◯ Wings or ◯ Nachos?

15. Would you rather eat

    ◯ 50 lbs of french fr███████ lbs of potato chips?

16. ○ Chocolate milk ○ Strawberry milk or ○ Plain milk?

17. ○ Hamburger or ○ Hot dog?

18. ○ Ketchup or ○ Mustard?

19. ○ Chunky peanut butter or ○ Creamy peanut butter?

20. Favorite cake? _____

21. Would you rather eat ○ Cookie dough or ○ Baked cookies?

22. ○ Sweet or ○ Tart?

23. Buffalo wings: ○ Mild or ○ Hot and spicy?

24. ○ Energy drinks or ○ Soda?

25. Favorite food of all time? _____

WARNING ~ Gross questions ahead!

26. Would you rather eat ○ Chocolate-covered ants or
    ○ Chocolate-covered worms?

27. ○ Roasted roaches or
    ○ Mashed-up maggots?

28. ○ Slime or ○ Boogers?

29. ○ Spaghetti with eyeballs or ○ Macaroni and guts?

30. Would you rather drink ○ A rotten banana milkshake or
    ○ A sour strawberry smoothie?

SPORTS REPORT

What's your score?

1. ○ Soccer or ○ Softball?

2. What sport do you play _____ or
   Wish you could _____?

3. ○ Superstar or ○ Benchwarmer?

4. ○ NFL ○ MLB ○ NHL
   ○ NBA ○ WNBA?

5. What's your favorite sports team?_____

6. Do you know the difference between a touchdown
   and a field goal? _____

7. Is a foul in basketball the same as a foul in baseball?
   ○ Sure thing. ○ No way! or ○ What's a foul?

8. ○ Die-hard fan or ○ Casual observer?

9. Watch a game ○ On TV or ○ In person?

10. ○ Read a book or ○ Jog around the block?

11. Are you more comfortable with ○ A bat or ○ A racket?

12. Ever pretended to be sick to get out of gym?
    ○ Never! or ○ Um, more than once!

13. Do you look forward to gym? ○ No way! or ○ Yes way!

14. Would you rather ○ Be pushed on little square
    scooters in gym class or ○ Be the one pushing?

15. ○ Dodgeball or ○ Volleyball?

16. ◯ Rope climbing or ◯ Obstacle course?

17. Would you rather watch ◯ ESPN or
◯ ABC Family?

18. Favorite indoor game? _____

19. ◯ Monopoly or ◯ Risk?

20. Would you rather ◯ Jump rope for an hour or
◯ Do push-ups for five minutes?

21. Would you rather swim in ◯ The ocean
◯ A lake or ◯ A pool?

22. ◯ Dive off the high dive ◯ Cannonball or
◯ There is no way you'd even climb the ladder?

23. Is riding a bike fun? _____

24. ◯ Hiking or ◯ Biking?

25. ◯ Rollerblade or ◯ Ice-skate?

26. Can you skateboard? _____

27. Do you know how to do an ollie? _____

28. Is cheerleading a sport? ◯ Absolutely!
◯ Absolutely not!

29. Can you do a herkie? ◯ Totally! ◯ Ouch!

30. Favorite Olympic event? _____

SPORTS REPORT

What's your score?

1. ◯ Soccer or ◯ Softball?

2. What sport do you play _____ or

   Wish you could _____ ?

3. ◯ Superstar or ◯ Benchwarmer?

4. ◯ NFL ◯ MLB ◯ NHL

   ◯ NBA ◯ WNBA?

5. What's your favorite sports team? _____

6. Do you know the difference between a touchdown

   and a field goal? _____

7. Is a foul in basketball the same as a foul in baseball?

   ◯ Sure thing. ◯ No way! or ◯ What's a foul?

8. ◯ Die-hard fan or ◯ Casual observer?

9. Watch a game ◯ On TV or ◯ In person?

10. ◯ Read a book or ◯ Jog around the block?

11. Are you more comfortable with ◯ A bat or ◯ A racket?

12. Ever pretended to be sick to get out of gym?

    ◯ Never! or ◯ Um, more than once!

13. Do you look forward to gym? ◯ No way! or ◯ Yes way!

14. Would you rather ◯ Be pushed on little square

    scooters in gym class or ◯ Be the one pushing?

15. ◯ Dodgeball or ◯ Volleyball?

16. ⭕ Rope climbing or ⭕ Obstacle course?

17. Would you rather watch ⭕ ESPN or ⭕ ABC Family?

18. Favorite indoor game? _____

19. ⭕ Monopoly or ⭕ Risk?

20. Would you rather ⭕ Jump rope for an hour or ⭕ Do push-ups for five minutes?

21. Would you rather swim in ⭕ The ocean ⭕ A lake or ⭕ A pool?

22. ⭕ Dive off the high dive ⭕ Cannonball or ⭕ There is no way you'd even climb the ladder?

23. Is riding a bike fun? _____

24. ⭕ Hiking or ⭕ Biking?

25. ⭕ Rollerblade or ⭕ Ice-skate?

26. Can you skateboard? _____

27. Do you know how to do an ollie? _____

28. Is cheerleading a sport? ⭕ Absolutely! ⭕ Absolutely not!

29. Can you do a herkie? ⭕ Totally! ⭕ Ouch!

30. Favorite Olympic event?_____

SPORTS REPORT

What's your score?

1. ◯ Soccer or ◯ Softball?

2. What sport do you play _____ or

   Wish you could _____?

3. ◯ Superstar or ◯ Benchwarmer?

4. ◯ NFL ◯ MLB ◯ NHL

   ◯ NBA ◯ WNBA?

5. What's your favorite sports team?_____

6. Do you know the difference between a touchdown

   and a field goal? _____

7. Is a foul in basketball the same as a foul in baseball?

   ◯ Sure thing. ◯ No way! or ◯ What's a foul?

8. ◯ Die-hard fan or ◯ Casual observer?

9. Watch a game ◯ On TV or ◯ In person?

10. ◯ Read a book or ◯ Jog around the block?

11. Are you more comfortable with ◯ A bat or ◯ A racket?

12. Ever pretended to be sick to get out of gym?

    ◯ Never! or ◯ Um, more than once!

13. Do you look forward to gym? ◯ No way! or ◯ Yes way!

14. Would you rather ◯ Be pushed on little square

    scooters in gym class or ◯ Be the one pushing?

15. ◯ Dodgeball or ◯ Volleyball?

16. ◯ Rope climbing or ◯ Obstacle course?

17. Would you rather watch ◯ ESPN or ◯ ABC Family?

18. Favorite indoor game? _____

19. ◯ Monopoly or ◯ Risk?

20. Would you rather ◯ Jump rope for an hour or ◯ Do push-ups for five minutes?

21. Would you rather swim in ◯ The ocean ◯ A lake or ◯ A pool?

22. ◯ Dive off the high dive ◯ Cannonball or ◯ There is no way you'd even climb the ladder?

23. Is riding a bike fun? _____

24. ◯ Hiking or ◯ Biking?

25. ◯ Rollerblade or ◯ Ice-skate?

26. Can you skateboard? _____

27. Do you know how to do an ollie? _____

28. Is cheerleading a sport? ◯ Absolutely! ◯ Absolutely not!

29. Can you do a herkie? ◯ Totally! ◯ Ouch!

30. Favorite Olympic event? _____

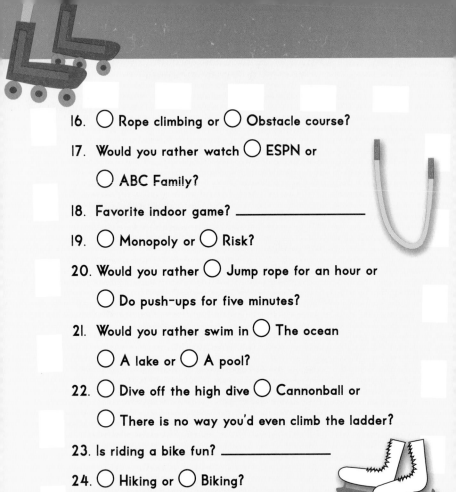

SPORTS REPORT

What's your score?

1. ⃝ Soccer or ⃝ Softball?

2. What sport do you play _____ or
   Wish you could _____?

3. ⃝ Superstar or ⃝ Benchwarmer?

4. ⃝ NFL ⃝ MLB ⃝ NHL
   ⃝ NBA ⃝ WNBA?

5 What's your favorite sports team?_____

6. Do you know the difference between a touchdown
   and a field goal? _____

7. Is a foul in basketball the same as a foul in baseball?
   ⃝ Sure thing. ⃝ No way! or ⃝ What's a foul?

8. ⃝ Die-hard fan or ⃝ Casual observer?

9. Watch a game ⃝ On TV or ⃝ In person?

10. ⃝ Read a book or ⃝ Jog around the block?

11. Are you more comfortable with ⃝ A bat or ⃝ A racket?

12. Ever pretended to be sick to get out of gym?
    ⃝ Never! or ⃝ Um, more than once!

13. Do you look forward to gym? ⃝ No way! or ⃝ Yes way!

14. Would you rather ⃝ Be pushed on little square
    scooters in gym class or ⃝ Be the one pushing?

15. ⃝ Dodgeball or ⃝ Volleyball?

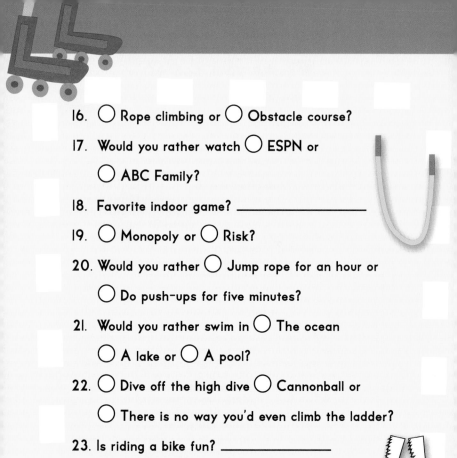

16. ◯ Rope climbing or ◯ Obstacle course?

17. Would you rather watch ◯ ESPN or
    ◯ ABC Family?

18. Favorite indoor game? _____

19. ◯ Monopoly or ◯ Risk?

20. Would you rather ◯ Jump rope for an hour or
    ◯ Do push-ups for five minutes?

21. Would you rather swim in ◯ The ocean
    ◯ A lake or ◯ A pool?

22. ◯ Dive off the high dive ◯ Cannonball or
    ◯ There is no way you'd even climb the ladder?

23. Is riding a bike fun? _____

24. ◯ Hiking or ◯ Biking?

25. ◯ Rollerblade or ◯ Ice-skate?

26. Can you skateboard? _____

27. Do you know how to do an ollie? _____

28. Is cheerleading a sport? ◯ Absolutely!
    ◯ Absolutely not!

29. Can you do a herkie? ◯ Totally! ◯ Ouch!

30. Favorite Olympic event? _____

FAMILY

Can't live with 'em, can't live without 'em!

1. ◯ Only child ◯ One of two ◯ One of many

2. If you're an Only, do you want siblings?

   ◯ Always ◯ Sometimes ◯ Never

   always

3. If you're one of many, do you want to be an Only?

   ◯ Never ◯ Sometimes ◯ Always

4. Do you have ◯ Brothers ◯ Sisters or ◯ Both?

5. Do you love your siblings ◯ Sometimes or

   ◯ All of the time?

   OMG!

6. Are your siblings ◯ Older ◯ Younger or ◯ Both?

7. Do you babysit a lot? _____

8. Are your parents ◯ Cool or ◯ OMG! You're kidding!?

9. Do your friends think your parents are cool?_____

10. Who would you want for celebrity parents? *NEVER!*

    _____

11. Do your parents embarrass you ◯ Sometimes

    ◯ Always ◯ Never?

    Cool

12. If so, how? _____

13. Do you know where your family is originally from?_____

    If yes, where? _____

14. Who's your favorite relative? _____

15. Why? _____ *Yes*

16. Does the rest of your family live ⚪ Close or ⚪ Far?

17. Do you have relatives who live with you? _____

18. If so, is that ⚪ Good or ⚪ Bad?

Brothers

19. Who pinches your cheek or asks you embarrassing questions? _____

20. Travel to ⚪ Hawaii with your grandparents or ⚪ The desert with your BFF?

SISTERS

21. ⚪ Hang out with your cousins on a cruise ship or ⚪ Go on a field trip with your class (and secret crush) to the art museum?

UGH!

22. Would you rather have ⚪ A huge family reunion or ⚪ A small family get-together?

Boring!

23. Do you see your cousins ⚪ Often ⚪ Rarely or ⚪ I don't have any cousins!

cousins

24. Are your cousins ⚪ Your age ⚪ Older or ⚪ Younger?

25. What is your full name? _____

26. Do you think it's ⚪ Boring or ⚪ Unique?

BFF

27. Are you named after someone? ⚪ Yes or ⚪ No

28. Did your parents have any other names picked out for you? If so, what? _____

29. Would you rather be called that? ⚪ Yes or ⚪ Ugh!

30. If you could choose your own name, what would you pick? _____

FAMILY

Can't live with 'em, can't live without 'em!

1. ○ Only child ○ One of two ○ One of many

2. If you're an Only, do you want siblings?

   ○ Always ○ Sometimes ○ Never

   always

3. If you're one of many, do you want to be an Only?

   ○ Never ○ Sometimes ○ Always

4. Do you have ○ Brothers ○ Sisters or ○ Both?

5. Do you love your siblings ○ Sometimes or

   ○ All of the time?

   OMG!

6. Are your siblings ○ Older ○ Younger or ○ Both?

7. Do you babysit a lot? _____

8. Are your parents ○ Cool or ○ OMG! You're kidding!?

9. Do your friends think your parents are cool?_____

10. Who would you want for celebrity parents? *NEVER!*

    _____

11. Do your parents embarrass you ○ Sometimes

    ○ Always ○ Never?

    Cool

12. If so, how? _____

13. Do you know where your family is originally from?_____

    If yes, where? _____

14. Who's your favorite relative? _____

15. Why? _____ *Yes*

16. Does the rest of your family live ◯ Close or ◯ Far?

17. Do you have relatives who live with you? _____

18. If so, is that ◯ Good or ◯ Bad?

Brothers

19. Who pinches your cheek or asks you embarrassing

    questions? _____

20. Travel to ◯ Hawaii with your grandparents or

    ◯ The desert with your BFF?

SISTERS

21. ◯ Hang out with your cousins on a cruise ship or

    ◯ Go on a field trip with your class (and secret

UGH! crush) to the art museum?

22. Would you rather have ◯ A huge family reunion

    or ◯ A small family get-together?

Boring!

23. Do you see your cousins ◯ Often ◯ Rarely or

    ◯ I don't have any cousins!

coresins

24. Are your cousins ◯ Your age ◯ Older or ◯ Younger?

25. What is your full name? _____

26. Do you think it's ◯ Boring or ◯ Unique?

BFF

27. Are you named after someone? ◯ Yes or ◯ No

28. Did your parents have any other names picked out

    for you? If so, what? _____

29. Would you rather be called that? ◯ Yes or ◯ Ugh!

30. If you could choose your own name, what would you

    pick? _____

FAMILY

Can't live with 'em, can't live without 'em!

1. ○ Only child ○ One of two ○ One of many

2. If you're an Only, do you want siblings?

   ○ Always ○ Sometimes ○ Never

   always

3. If you're one of many, do you want to be an Only?

   ○ Never ○ Sometimes ○ Always

4. Do you have ○ Brothers ○ Sisters or ○ Both?

5. Do you love your siblings ○ Sometimes or

   ○ All of the time?

   OMG!

6. Are your siblings ○ Older ○ Younger or ○ Both?

7. Do you babysit a lot? _____

8. Are your parents ○ Cool or ○ OMG! You're kidding!?

9. Do your friends think your parents are cool?_____

10. Who would you want for celebrity parents? *NEVER!*

    _____

11. Do your parents embarrass you ○ Sometimes

    ○ Always ○ Never?

    Cool

12. If so, how? _____

13. Do you know where your family is originally from?_____

    If yes, where? _____

14. Who's your favorite relative? _____

15. Why? _____ *Yes*

16. Does the rest of your family live ◯ Close or ◯ Far?

17. Do you have relatives who live with you? _____

18. If so, is that ◯ Good or ◯ Bad?

Brothers

19. Who pinches your cheek or asks you embarrassing

    questions? _____

20. Travel to ◯ Hawaii with your grandparents or

    ◯ The desert with your BFF?

SISTERS

21. ◯ Hang out with your cousins on a cruise ship or

    ◯ Go on a field trip with your class (and secret

UGH! crush) to the art museum?

22. Would you rather have ◯ A huge family reunion

    or ◯ A small family get-together?

Boring!

23. Do you see your cousins ◯ Often ◯ Rarely or

    ◯ I don't have any cousins!

cousins

24. Are your cousins ◯ Your age ◯ Older or ◯ Younger?

25. What is your full name? _____

26. Do you think it's ◯ Boring or ◯ Unique?

BFF

27. Are you named after someone? ◯ Yes or ◯ No

28. Did your parents have any other names picked out

    for you? If so, what? _____

29. Would you rather be called that? ◯ Yes or ◯ Ugh!

30. If you could choose your own name, what would you

    pick? _____

FAMILY

Can't live with 'em, can't live without 'em!

1. ⬭ Only child ⬭ One of two ⬭ One of many

2. If you're an Only, do you want siblings?

   ⬭ Always ⬭ Sometimes ⬭ Never   *always*

3. If you're one of many, do you want to be an Only?

   ⬭ Never ⬭ Sometimes ⬭ Always

4. Do you have ⬭ Brothers ⬭ Sisters or ⬭ Both?

5. Do you love your siblings ⬭ Sometimes or

   ⬭ All of the time?   *OMG!*

6. Are your siblings ⬭ Older ⬭ Younger or ⬭ Both?

7. Do you babysit a lot? _____

8. Are your parents ⬭ Cool or ⬭ OMG! You're kidding!?

9. Do your friends think your parents are cool?_____

10. Who would you want for celebrity parents? *NEVER!*

    _____

11. Do your parents embarrass you ⬭ Sometimes

    ⬭ Always ⬭ Never?   *Cool*

12. If so, how? _____

13. Do you know where your family is originally from?____

    If yes, where? _____

14. Who's your favorite relative? _____

15. Why? _____   *Yes*

16. Does the rest of your family live ◯ Close or ◯ Far?

17. Do you have relatives who live with you? _____

18. If so, is that ◯ Good or ◯ Bad?

Brothers

19. Who pinches your cheek or asks you embarrassing

    questions? _____

20. Travel to ◯ Hawaii with your grandparents or

    ◯ The desert with your BFF?

SISTERS

21. ◯ Hang out with your cousins on a cruise ship or

    ◯ Go on a field trip with your class (and secret

    crush) to the art museum?

UGH!

22. Would you rather have ◯ A huge family reunion

    or ◯ A small family get-together?

Boring!

23. Do you see your cousins ◯ Often ◯ Rarely or

    ◯ I don't have any cousins!

cousins

24. Are your cousins ◯ Your age ◯ Older or ◯ Younger?

25. What is your full name? _____

26. Do you think it's ◯ Boring or ◯ Unique?

BFF

27. Are you named after someone? ◯ Yes or ◯ No

28. Did your parents have any other names picked out

    for you? If so, what? _____

29. Would you rather be called that? ◯ Yes or ◯ Ugh!

30. If you could choose your own name, what would you

    pick? _____

PERSONALITY POP QUIZ
Who are you?

1. Are you ◯ Quiet or ◯ Loud?

2. ◯ Moody or ◯ A pocketful of sunshine?

3. Do you think before you speak ◯ Too much or

   ◯ Not at all?

4. ◯ Splash through the puddles or

   ◯ Walk carefully around them?

5. ◯ Do you like to gossip or

   ◯ Are you good at keeping a secret?

6. Do you ◯ Look on the bright side of things or

   ◯ Worry about the future?

7. ◯ Fraidy cat or ◯ Fearless?

8. What scares you the most?_____

9. What makes you laugh? _____

10. ◯ Giggle or ◯ Guffaw?

11. ◯ Share your feelings or ◯ Keep them to yourself?

12. Would you rather ◯ Go bungee jumping or

   ◯ Knit a sweater?

13. ◯ Go to the movies or ◯ Rent a DVD?

14. Which movies or books made you cry?_____
_____

15. Have you ever told a white lie (or worse)?_____

16. ⭘ Dawn or ⭘ Twilight?

17. ⭘ Rain or ⭘ Shine?

18. Would you rather ⭘ Be a millionaire for five years or ⭘ Be poor and live forever?

19. ⭘ Wear a clown costume to school every day for a year or ⭘ Eat lunch with the dorkiest kid in your class every day for the rest of the year?

20. ⭘ Never have dessert again or ⭘ Never watch TV again?

21. ⭘ Boarding school or ⭘ Home school?

22. ⭘ Gourmet cook or ⭘ Kitchen disaster?

23. ⭘ Read a book or ⭘ Play on the computer?

24. ⭘ Make people laugh or ⭘ Be the one laughing?

25. What's your pet peeve? _____

26. Would you rather dress up as ⭘ A witch or ⭘ A princess?

27. ⭘ Vampire or ⭘ Werewolf?

28. ⭘ Cinderella or ⭘ Sleeping Beauty?

29. ⭘ Evil Stepmother or ⭘ Wicked Fairy?

30. What's the best Halloween costume you've ever worn? _____

PERSONALITY POP QUIZ
Who are you?

1. Are you ◯ Quiet or ◯ Loud?

2. ◯ Moody or ◯ A pocketful of sunshine?

3. Do you think before you speak ◯ Too much or
   ◯ Not at all?

4. ◯ Splash through the puddles or
   ◯ Walk carefully around them?

5. ◯ Do you like to gossip or
   ◯ Are you good at keeping a secret?

6. Do you ◯ Look on the bright side of things or
   ◯ Worry about the future?

7. ◯ Fraidy cat or ◯ Fearless?

8. What scares you the most?_____

9. What makes you laugh? _____

10. ◯ Giggle or ◯ Guffaw?

11. ◯ Share your feelings or ◯ Keep them to yourself?

12. Would you rather ◯ Go bungee jumping or
    ◯ Knit a sweater?

13. ◯ Go to the movies or ◯ Rent a DVD?

14. Which movies or books made you cry?_____
    _____

15. Have you ever told a white lie (or worse)?_____

16. ○ Dawn or ○ Twilight?

17. ○ Rain or ○ Shine?

18. Would you rather ○ Be a millionaire for five years or ○ Be poor and live forever?

19. ○ Wear a clown costume to school every day for a year or ○ Eat lunch with the dorkiest kid in your class every day for the rest of the year?

20. ○ Never have dessert again or ○ Never watch TV again?

21. ○ Boarding school or ○ Home school?

22. ○ Gourmet cook or ○ Kitchen disaster?

23. ○ Read a book or ○ Play on the computer?

24. ○ Make people laugh or ○ Be the one laughing?

25. What's your pet peeve? _____

26. Would you rather dress up as ○ A witch or ○ A princess?

27. ○ Vampire or ○ Werewolf?

28. ○ Cinderella or ○ Sleeping Beauty?

29. ○ Evil Stepmother or ○ Wicked Fairy?

30. What's the best Halloween costume you've ever worn? _____

PERSONALITY POP QUIZ
Who are you?

1. Are you ○ Quiet or ○ Loud?

2. ○ Moody or ○ A pocketful of sunshine?

3. Do you think before you speak ○ Too much or
   ○ Not at all?

4. ○ Splash through the puddles or
   ○ Walk carefully around them?

5. ○ Do you like to gossip or
   ○ Are you good at keeping a secret?

6. Do you ○ Look on the bright side of things or
   ○ Worry about the future?

7. ○ Fraidy cat or ○ Fearless?

8. What scares you the most?_____

9. What makes you laugh? _____

10. ○ Giggle or ○ Guffaw?

11. ○ Share your feelings or ○ Keep them to yourself?

12. Would you rather ○ Go bungee jumping or
    ○ Knit a sweater?

13. ○ Go to the movies or ○ Rent a DVD?

14. Which movies or books made you cry?_____
    _____

15. Have you ever told a white lie (or worse)?_____

16. ◯ Dawn or ◯ Twilight?

17. ◯ Rain or ◯ Shine?

18. Would you rather ◯ Be a millionaire for five years or ◯ Be poor and live forever?

19. ◯ Wear a clown costume to school every day for a year or ◯ Eat lunch with the dorkiest kid in your class every day for the rest of the year?

20. ◯ Never have dessert again or ◯ Never watch TV again?

21. ◯ Boarding school or ◯ Home school?

22. ◯ Gourmet cook or ◯ Kitchen disaster?

23. ◯ Read a book or ◯ Play on the computer?

24. ◯ Make people laugh or ◯ Be the one laughing?

25. What's your pet peeve? _____

26. Would you rather dress up as ◯ A witch or ◯ A princess?

27. ◯ Vampire or ◯ Werewolf?

28. ◯ Cinderella or ◯ Sleeping Beauty?

29. ◯ Evil Stepmother or ◯ Wicked Fairy?

30. What's the best Halloween costume you've ever worn? _____

PERSONALITY POP QUIZ
Who are you?

1. Are you ◯ Quiet or ◯ Loud?

2. ◯ Moody or ◯ A pocketful of sunshine?

3. Do you think before you speak ◯ Too much or
   ◯ Not at all?

4. ◯ Splash through the puddles or
   ◯ Walk carefully around them?

5. ◯ Do you like to gossip or
   ◯ Are you good at keeping a secret?

6. Do you ◯ Look on the bright side of things or
   ◯ Worry about the future?

7. ◯ Fraidy cat or ◯ Fearless?

8. What scares you the most?_____

9. What makes you laugh? _____

10. ◯ Giggle or ◯ Guffaw?

11. ◯ Share your feelings or ◯ Keep them to yourself?

12. Would you rather ◯ Go bungee jumping or
    ◯ Knit a sweater?

13. ◯ Go to the movies or ◯ Rent a DVD?

14. Which movies or books made you cry?_____
_____

15. Have you ever told a white lie (or worse)?_____

16. ⃝ Dawn or ⃝ Twilight?

17. ⃝ Rain or ⃝ Shine?

18. Would you rather ⃝ Be a millionaire for five years or ⃝ Be poor and live forever?

19. ⃝ Wear a clown costume to school every day for a year or ⃝ Eat lunch with the dorkiest kid in your class every day for the rest of the year?

20. ⃝ Never have dessert again or ⃝ Never watch TV again?

21. ⃝ Boarding school or ⃝ Home school?

22. ⃝ Gourmet cook or ⃝ Kitchen disaster?

23. ⃝ Read a book or ⃝ Play on the computer?

24. ⃝ Make people laugh or ⃝ Be the one laughing?

25. What's your pet peeve? _____

26. Would you rather dress up as ⃝ A witch or ⃝ A princess?

27. ⃝ Vampire or ⃝ Werewolf?

28. ⃝ Cinderella or ⃝ Sleeping Beauty?

29. ⃝ Evil Stepmother or ⃝ Wicked Fairy?

30. What's the best Halloween costume you've ever worn? _____

MUSIC TO YOUR EARS

Your personal playlist

1. Favorite artist? _____

2. ◯ Rap ◯ Rock ◯ Jazz ◯ Classical ◯ Pop
   or ◯ Country?

3. Favorite song right now?_____

4. Favorite song ever? _____

5. What song are you sick of hearing?_____

6. Favorite music video? _____

7. What video are you sick of seeing? _____

8. Who is THE most popular band now? _____

9. Who is the artist EVERYONE likes? _____

10. Do you like them? ◯ Yes ◯ No or ◯ A little

11. Do you prefer ◯ Girl groups or ◯ Boy bands?

12. ◯ Download music or ◯ Buy CDs?

13. ◯ Songs that make you dance or
    ◯ Songs that make you cry?

14. Do you play an instrument? _____

15. Which one(s)? _____

16. If not, which instrument would you want to play?

   _____

17. ○ Marching band or ○ Rock band?

18. What would the name of your band be? _____

19. Which instrument would drive your parents crazier?

   ○ Electric guitar or ○ Drums?

20. Do you like to dance? _____

21. Can you dance the cha-cha-cha? _____

22. Who would you want to dance with? _____

23. ○ Sing in the shower or ○ Sing anytime, anywhere?

24. ○ Radio or ○ MP3 player?

25. Would you rather be ○ A professional singer or

   ○ A professional dancer?

26. Would you want to be a backup singer or dancer?

   ○ Not so much. ○ Yes, I would!

27. Who's the best dancer in your class? _____

28. Who's the best singer in your class? _____

29. Would you rather go to a ○ Rock concert or

   ○ Country music show?

30. What band would you want to join on

   stage? _____

MUSIC TO YOUR EARS

Your personal playlist

1. Favorite artist? _____

2. ○ Rap ○ Rock ○ Jazz ○ Classical ○ Pop
   or ○ Country?

3. Favorite song right now?_____

4. Favorite song ever? _____

5. What song are you sick of hearing?_____

6. Favorite music video? _____

7. What video are you sick of seeing? _____

8. Who is THE most popular band now? _____

9. Who is the artist EVERYONE likes? _____

10. Do you like them? ○ Yes ○ No or ○ A little

11. Do you prefer ○ Girl groups or ○ Boy bands?

12. ○ Download music or ○ Buy CDs?

13. ○ Songs that make you dance or
    ○ Songs that make you cry?

14. Do you play an instrument? _____

15. Which one(s)? _____

16. If not, which instrument would you want to play?

_____

17. ◯ Marching band or ◯ Rock band?

18. What would the name of your band be? _____

19. Which instrument would drive your parents crazier?

◯ Electric guitar or ◯ Drums?

20. Do you like to dance? _____

21. Can you dance the cha-cha-cha? _____

22. Who would you want to dance with? _____

23. ◯ Sing in the shower or ◯ Sing anytime, anywhere?

24. ◯ Radio or ◯ MP3 player?

25. Would you rather be ◯ A professional singer or

◯ A professional dancer?

26. Would you want to be a backup singer or dancer?

◯ Not so much. ◯ Yes, I would!

27. Who's the best dancer in your class? _____

28. Who's the best singer in your class? _____

29. Would you rather go to a ◯ Rock concert or

◯ Country music show?

30. What band would you want to join on

stage? _____

MUSIC TO YOUR EARS

Your personal playlist

1. Favorite artist? _____

2. ○ Rap ○ Rock ○ Jazz ○ Classical ○ Pop

   or ○ Country?

3. Favorite song right now?_____

4. Favorite song ever? _____

5. What song are you sick of hearing?_____

6. Favorite music video? _____

7. What video are you sick of seeing? _____

8. Who is THE most popular band now? _____

9. Who is the artist EVERYONE likes? _____

10. Do you like them? ○ Yes ○ No or ○ A little

11. Do you prefer ○ Girl groups or ○ Boy bands?

12. ○ Download music or ○ Buy CDs?

13. ○ Songs that make you dance or

    ○ Songs that make you cry?

14. Do you play an instrument? _____

15. Which one(s)? _____

16. If not, which instrument would you want to play?

_____

17. ◯ Marching band or ◯ Rock band?

18. What would the name of your band be? _____

19. Which instrument would drive your parents crazier?

◯ Electric guitar or ◯ Drums?

20. Do you like to dance? _____

21. Can you dance the cha-cha-cha? _____

22. Who would you want to dance with? _____

23. ◯ Sing in the shower or ◯ Sing anytime, anywhere?

24. ◯ Radio or ◯ MP3 player?

25. Would you rather be ◯ A professional singer or

◯ A professional dancer?

26. Would you want to be a backup singer or dancer?

◯ Not so much. ◯ Yes, I would!

27. Who's the best dancer in your class? _____

28. Who's the best singer in your class? _____

29. Would you rather go to a ◯ Rock concert or

◯ Country music show?

30. What band would you want to join on

stage? _____

MUSIC TO YOUR EARS

Your personal playlist

1. Favorite artist? _____

2. ◯ Rap ◯ Rock ◯ Jazz ◯ Classical ◯ Pop

   or ◯ Country?

3. Favorite song right now?_____

4. Favorite song ever? _____

5. What song are you sick of hearing?_____

6. Favorite music video? _____

7. What video are you sick of seeing? _____

8. Who is THE most popular band now? _____

9. Who is the artist EVERYONE likes? _____

10. Do you like them? ◯ Yes ◯ No or ◯ A little

11. Do you prefer ◯ Girl groups or ◯ Boy bands?

12. ◯ Download music or ◯ Buy CDs?

13. ◯ Songs that make you dance or

    ◯ Songs that make you cry?

14. Do you play an instrument? _____

15. Which one(s)? _____

16. If not, which instrument would you want to play?

_____

17. ○ Marching band or ○ Rock band?

18. What would the name of your band be? _____

19. Which instrument would drive your parents crazier?

○ Electric guitar or ○ Drums?

20. Do you like to dance? _____

21. Can you dance the cha-cha-cha? _____

22. Who would you want to dance with? _____

23. ○ Sing in the shower or ○ Sing anytime, anywhere?

24. ○ Radio or ○ MP3 player?

25. Would you rather be ○ A professional singer or

○ A professional dancer?

26. Would you want to be a backup singer or dancer?

○ Not so much. ○ Yes, I would!

27. Who's the best dancer in your class? _____

28. Who's the best singer in your class? _____

29. Would you rather go to a ○ Rock concert or

○ Country music show?

30. What band would you want to join on

stage? _____

Celeb Central
Which stars are in your eyes?

1. Favorite male movie actor? _____

2. Favorite female movie actor? _____

3. Would you rather ◯ Star in a movie with your favorite actor or ◯ Go to a nice dinner with them?

4. Who is old news? _____

5. Do you look like any celebrity? ◯ Absolutely! ◯ Are you kidding?

6. If yes, who? _____

7. Who do you want to look like? _____

8. Which actor—living or dead—would you want to meet? _____

9. Which celeb do you think is an all-time hottie? _____

10. Would a movie of your life be:
    ◯ An action-adventure ◯ A slapstick comedy or
    ◯ An Oscar-winning drama?

11. Who would play you? _____

12. Who would play your best friend? _____

13. What is your favorite movie of all time? _____

14. ◯ Comedy or ◯ Scary movie?

15. ◯ Love story or ◯ Adventure?

16. Favorite sappy movie? _____

17. Favorite funny film? _____

18. Favorite scary movie? _____

19. Do you ◯ Hide your eyes at the scary parts or

    ◯ Watch all the gory details?

20. ◯ Fantasy or ◯ Real life?

21. First movie you saw in a theater? _____

22. What TV show can you not miss? _____

23. What TV show makes you laugh because it's funny?

    _____

24. Because it's dumb? _____

25. Favorite TV mom? _____

26. Favorite TV dad? _____

27. What TV show would you love to star in?

    _____

28. If you could create a TV show, what would you call

    it? _____

29. Would you rather ◯ Watch TV or ◯ Read a book?

30. ◯ Sit in front of the TV all day or ◯ Spend all

    day at the movies?

Celeb Central
Which stars are in your eyes?

1. Favorite male movie actor? _____

2. Favorite female movie actor? _____

3. Would you rather ○ Star in a movie with your favorite actor or ○ Go to a nice dinner with them?

4. Who is old news? _____

5. Do you look like any celebrity? ○ Absolutely!
   ○ Are you kidding?

6. If yes, who? _____

7. Who do you want to look like? _____

8. Which actor—living or dead—would you want to meet?
   _____

9. Which celeb do you think is an all-time hottie?
   _____

10. Would a movie of your life be:
    ○ An action-adventure ○ A slapstick comedy or
    ○ An Oscar-winning drama?

11. Who would play you? _____

12. Who would play your best friend? _____

13. What is your favorite movie of all time? _____
    _____

14. ○ Comedy or ○ Scary movie?

15. ○ Love story or ○ Adventure?

16. Favorite sappy movie? _____

17. Favorite funny film? _____

18. Favorite scary movie? _____

19. Do you ◯ Hide your eyes at the scary parts or

    ◯ Watch all the gory details?

20. ◯ Fantasy or ◯ Real life?

21. First movie you saw in a theater? _____

22. What TV show can you not miss? _____

23. What TV show makes you laugh because it's funny?

    _____

24. Because it's dumb? _____

25. Favorite TV mom? _____

26. Favorite TV dad? _____

27. What TV show would you love to star in?

    _____

28. If you could create a TV show, what would you call

    it? _____

29. Would you rather ◯ Watch TV or ◯ Read a book?

30. ◯ Sit in front of the TV all day or ◯ Spend all

    day at the movies?

Celeb Central

Which stars are in your eyes?

1. Favorite male movie actor? _____

2. Favorite female movie actor? _____

3. Would you rather ○ Star in a movie with your favorite actor or ○ Go to a nice dinner with them?

4. Who is old news? _____

5. Do you look like any celebrity? ○ Absolutely!
   ○ Are you kidding?

6. If yes, who? _____

7. Who do you want to look like? _____

8. Which actor—living or dead—would you want to meet?
   _____

9. Which celeb do you think is an all-time hottie?
   _____

10. Would a movie of your life be:
    ○ An action-adventure ○ A slapstick comedy or
    ○ An Oscar-winning drama?

11. Who would play you? _____

12. Who would play your best friend? _____

13. What is your favorite movie of all time? _____
    _____

14. ○ Comedy or ○ Scary movie?

15. ○ Love story or ○ Adventure?

16. Favorite sappy movie? _____

17. Favorite funny film? _____

18. Favorite scary movie? _____

19. Do you ◯ Hide your eyes at the scary parts or

◯ Watch all the gory details?

20. ◯ Fantasy or ◯ Real life?

21. First movie you saw in a theater? _____

22. What TV show can you not miss? _____

23. What TV show makes you laugh because it's funny?

_____

24. Because it's dumb? _____

25. Favorite TV mom? _____

26. Favorite TV dad? _____

27. What TV show would you love to star in?

_____

28. If you could create a TV show, what would you call

it? _____

29. Would you rather ◯ Watch TV or ◯ Read a book?

30. ◯ Sit in front of the TV all day or ◯ Spend all

day at the movies?

Celeb Central

Which stars are in your eyes?

1. Favorite male movie actor? _____

2. Favorite female movie actor? _____

3. Would you rather ⚪ Star in a movie with your favorite actor or ⚪ Go to a nice dinner with them?

4. Who is old news? _____

5. Do you look like any celebrity? ⚪ Absolutely! ⚪ Are you kidding?

6. If yes, who? _____

7. Who do you want to look like? _____

8. Which actor—living or dead—would you want to meet? _____

9. Which celeb do you think is an all-time hottie? _____

10. Would a movie of your life be:
    ⚪ An action-adventure ⚪ A slapstick comedy or
    ⚪ An Oscar-winning drama?

11. Who would play you? _____

12. Who would play your best friend? _____

13. What is your favorite movie of all time? _____

14. ⚪ Comedy or ⚪ Scary movie?

15. ⚪ Love story or ⚪ Adventure?

16. Favorite sappy movie? _____

17. Favorite funny film?_____

18. Favorite scary movie? _____

19. Do you ◯ Hide your eyes at the scary parts or

◯ Watch all the gory details?

20. ◯ Fantasy or ◯ Real life?

21. First movie you saw in a theater?_____

22. What TV show can you not miss?_____

23. What TV show makes you laugh because it's funny?

_____

24. Because it's dumb? _____

25. Favorite TV mom? _____

26. Favorite TV dad? _____

27. What TV show would you love to star in?

_____

28. If you could create a TV show, what would you call

it? _____

29. Would you rather ◯ Watch TV or ◯ Read a book?

30. ◯ Sit in front of the TV all day or ◯ Spend all

day at the movies?

WHEN I GROW UP...

WHAT DOES YOUR FUTURE HOLD?

1. Do you want to ⚪ Go to college or

   ⚪ Get a job right away?

2. Where?_____

3. ⚪ Lawyer ⚪ Doctor ⚪ Deep-sea diver

   ⚪ Astronaut ⚪ Other_____?

4. Because of you, ⚪ World hunger is eliminated or

   ⚪ All orphans are adopted?

5. If you could find a cure for only one disease,

   what would it be? ⚪ Cancer ⚪ Diabetes or

   ⚪ Heart disease?

6. Would you rather be a ⚪ Firefighter or ⚪ Police officer?

7. ⚪ EMT or ⚪ Fashion Designer?

8. ⚪ President or ⚪ Poet?

9. ⚪ Sports star or ⚪ Movie star?

10. Would you rather ⚪ Edit books or ⚪ Write them?

11. ⚪ Write songs or ⚪ Sing them?

12. Would you rather travel the world by ⚪ Plane or ⚪ Train?

13. Would you rather live ⚪ In the country or ⚪ In the city?

14. ⚪ In a penthouse apartment or ⚪ In a mansion?

15. ⚪ Luxury houseboat off the Florida Keys or ⚪ Really

    cool tree house somewhere in Alaska?

16. ⬤ By the beach or ⬤ In the mountains?

17. What country would you live in?_____

18. What city would you want to live in?_____

19. Best place to vacation? _____

20. Would you rather ⬤ Take a four-day cruise or

⬤ Stay on an island for a week?

21. ⬤ Spend a lazy day at the beach or

⬤ Sightsee to your heart's content?

22. Would you rather live ⬤ Near your parents or

⬤ Far, far away?

23. Do you want to ⬤ Get married or ⬤ Be single?

24. How many kids do you want? _____

25. ⬤ Boys ⬤ Girls or ⬤ Both?

26. Will you have ⬤ Lots of pets or ⬤ None?

27. ⬤ Private jet or ⬤ Limousine?

28. Would you rather ⬤ Drive yourself or ⬤ Have a chauffeur?

29. Would you rather be ⬤ Stranded on a deserted island or

⬤ Stuck on a mountaintop?

30. Would you rather live ⬤ On Mars or ⬤ Under the sea?

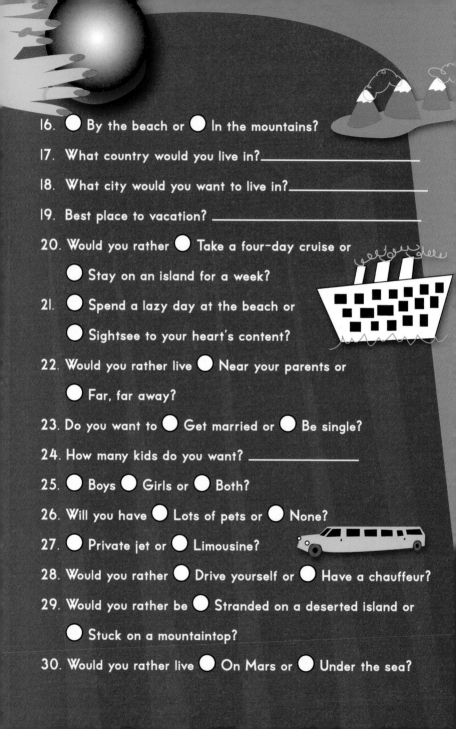

WHEN I GROW UP...

WHAT DOES YOUR FUTURE HOLD?

1. Do you want to ⬤ Go to college or

   ⬤ Get a job right away?

2. Where?_____

3. ⬤ Lawyer ⬤ Doctor ⬤ Deep-sea diver

   ⬤ Astronaut ⬤ Other_____?

4. Because of you, ⬤ World hunger is eliminated or

   ⬤ All orphans are adopted?

5. If you could find a cure for only one disease,

   what would it be? ⬤ Cancer ⬤ Diabetes or

   ⬤ Heart disease?

6. Would you rather be a ⬤ Firefighter or ⬤ Police officer?

7. ⬤ EMT or ⬤ Fashion Designer?

8. ⬤ President or ⬤ Poet?

9. ⬤ Sports star or ⬤ Movie star?

10. Would you rather ⬤ Edit books or ⬤ Write them?

11. ⬤ Write songs or ⬤ Sing them?

12. Would you rather travel the world by ⬤ Plane or ⬤ Train?

13. Would you rather live ⬤ In the country or ⬤ In the city?

14. ⬤ In a penthouse apartment or ⬤ In a mansion?

15. ⬤ Luxury houseboat off the Florida Keys or ⬤ Really

    cool tree house somewhere in Alaska?

16. ⚪ By the beach or ⚪ In the mountains?

17. What country would you live in?_____

18. What city would you want to live in?_____

19. Best place to vacation? _____

20. Would you rather ⚪ Take a four-day cruise or

    ⚪ Stay on an island for a week?

21. ⚪ Spend a lazy day at the beach or

    ⚪ Sightsee to your heart's content?

22. Would you rather live ⚪ Near your parents or

    ⚪ Far, far away?

23. Do you want to ⚪ Get married or ⚪ Be single?

24. How many kids do you want? _____

25. ⚪ Boys ⚪ Girls or ⚪ Both?

26. Will you have ⚪ Lots of pets or ⚪ None?

27. ⚪ Private jet or ⚪ Limousine?

28. Would you rather ⚪ Drive yourself or ⚪ Have a chauffeur?

29. Would you rather be ⚪ Stranded on a deserted island or

    ⚪ Stuck on a mountaintop?

30. Would you rather live ⚪ On Mars or ⚪ Under the sea?

WHEN I GROW UP...

WHAT DOES YOUR FUTURE HOLD?

1. Do you want to ○ Go to college or
   ○ Get a job right away?

2. Where?_____

3. ○ Lawyer ○ Doctor ○ Deep-sea diver
   ○ Astronaut ○ Other_____?

4. Because of you, ○ World hunger is eliminated or
   ○ All orphans are adopted?

5. If you could find a cure for only one disease,
   what would it be? ○ Cancer ○ Diabetes or
   ○ Heart disease?

6. Would you rather be a ○ Firefighter or ○ Police officer?

7. ○ EMT or ○ Fashion Designer?

8. ○ President or ○ Poet?

9. ○ Sports star or ○ Movie star?

10. Would you rather ○ Edit books or ○ Write them?

11. ○ Write songs or ○ Sing them?

12. Would you rather travel the world by ○ Plane or ○ Train?

13. Would you rather live ○ In the country or ○ In the city?

14. ○ In a penthouse apartment or ○ In a mansion?

15. ○ Luxury houseboat off the Florida Keys or ○ Really
    cool tree house somewhere in Alaska?

16. ⚪ By the beach or ⚪ In the mountains?

17. What country would you live in?_____

18. What city would you want to live in?_____

19. Best place to vacation? _____

20. Would you rather ⚪ Take a four-day cruise or ⚪ Stay on an island for a week?

21. ⚪ Spend a lazy day at the beach or ⚪ Sightsee to your heart's content?

22. Would you rather live ⚪ Near your parents or ⚪ Far, far away?

23. Do you want to ⚪ Get married or ⚪ Be single?

24. How many kids do you want? _____

25. ⚪ Boys ⚪ Girls or ⚪ Both?

26. Will you have ⚪ Lots of pets or ⚪ None?

27. ⚪ Private jet or ⚪ Limousine?

28. Would you rather ⚪ Drive yourself or ⚪ Have a chauffeur?

29. Would you rather be ⚪ Stranded on a deserted island or ⚪ Stuck on a mountaintop?

30. Would you rather live ⚪ On Mars or ⚪ Under the sea?

WHEN I GROW UP...

WHAT DOES YOUR FUTURE HOLD?

1. Do you want to ⚪ Go to college or

   ⚪ Get a job right away?

2. Where?_____

3. ⚪ Lawyer ⚪ Doctor ⚪ Deep-sea diver

   ⚪ Astronaut ⚪ Other_____?

4. Because of you, ⚪ World hunger is eliminated or

   ⚪ All orphans are adopted?

5. If you could find a cure for only one disease,

   what would it be? ⚪ Cancer ⚪ Diabetes or

   ⚪ Heart disease?

6. Would you rather be a ⚪ Firefighter or ⚪ Police officer?

7. ⚪ EMT or ⚪ Fashion Designer?

8. ⚪ President or ⚪ Poet?

9. ⚪ Sports star or ⚪ Movie star?

10. Would you rather ⚪ Edit books or ⚪ Write them?

11. ⚪ Write songs or ⚪ Sing them?

12. Would you rather travel the world by ⚪ Plane or ⚪ Train?

13. Would you rather live ⚪ In the country or ⚪ In the city?

14. ⚪ In a penthouse apartment or ⚪ In a mansion?

15. ⚪ Luxury houseboat off the Florida Keys or ⚪ Really

    cool tree house somewhere in Alaska?

16. ⚪ By the beach or ⚪ In the mountains?

17. What country would you live in?_____

18. What city would you want to live in?_____

19. Best place to vacation? _____

20. Would you rather ⚪ Take a four-day cruise or

    ⚪ Stay on an island for a week?

21. ⚪ Spend a lazy day at the beach or

    ⚪ Sightsee to your heart's content?

22. Would you rather live ⚪ Near your parents or

    ⚪ Far, far away?

23. Do you want to ⚪ Get married or ⚪ Be single?

24. How many kids do you want? _____

25. ⚪ Boys ⚪ Girls or ⚪ Both?

26. Will you have ⚪ Lots of pets or ⚪ None?

27. ⚪ Private jet or ⚪ Limousine?

28. Would you rather ⚪ Drive yourself or ⚪ Have a chauffeur?

29. Would you rather be ⚪ Stranded on a deserted island or

    ⚪ Stuck on a mountaintop?

30. Would you rather live ⚪ On Mars or ⚪ Under the sea?

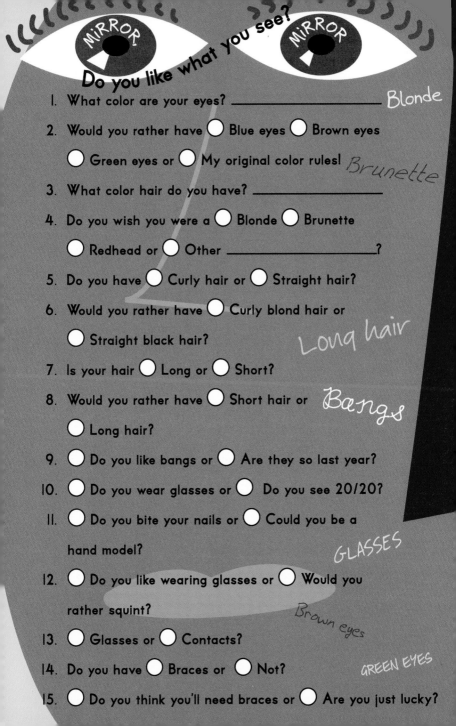

Do you like what you see?

1. What color are your eyes? _____ *Blonde*

2. Would you rather have ⚪ Blue eyes ⚪ Brown eyes
   ⚪ Green eyes or ⚪ My original color rules! *Brunette*

3. What color hair do you have? _____

4. Do you wish you were a ⚪ Blonde ⚪ Brunette
   ⚪ Redhead or ⚪ Other _____?

5. Do you have ⚪ Curly hair or ⚪ Straight hair?

6. Would you rather have ⚪ Curly blond hair or
   ⚪ Straight black hair? *Long hair*

7. Is your hair ⚪ Long or ⚪ Short?

8. Would you rather have ⚪ Short hair or *Bangs*
   ⚪ Long hair?

9. ⚪ Do you like bangs or ⚪ Are they so last year?

10. ⚪ Do you wear glasses or ⚪ Do you see 20/20?

11. ⚪ Do you bite your nails or ⚪ Could you be a
    hand model? *GLASSES*

12. ⚪ Do you like wearing glasses or ⚪ Would you
    rather squint? *Brown eyes*

13. ⚪ Glasses or ⚪ Contacts?

14. Do you have ⚪ Braces or ⚪ Not? *GREEN EYES*

15. ⚪ Do you think you'll need braces or ⚪ Are you just lucky?

16. ○ Silver braces or ○ The almost invisible, clear plastic kind?

Silver

17. Would you ever wear colored contacts? ○ Yes! ○ No!

18. Are you ○ Too tall? ○ Too short? ○ Just right?

Tall

19. Would you rather be ○ Too tall or ○ Too Short?

Short

20. Do you consider your voice ○ High and squeaky? ○ Low and husky? or ○ In the middle?

Legs

21. Do you like your knees? ○ They're OK. ○ Too knobby.

22. Do you have ○ Long legs or ○ Short legs?

23. Do you think your nose is ○ Too big? ○ Too small? ○ Just right?

24. Do you like freckles? ○ They're not so bad in moderation. ○ Ew, get me the lemon juice!

GIRLY-GIRL

25. What's your shoe size? _____

tomboy

26. Do you like your feet? ○ Yes! ○ No or ○ Never thought about them!

27. Do you keep your toenails painted? ○ Always! or ○ Nope. It doesn't matter to me.

JUST RIGHT

28. Do you ○ Tan or ○ Burn?

29. Are you ○ A tomboy or ○ A girly-girl?

30. Do you prefer your clothes ○ Baggy or ○ Form-fitting?

MiRROR MiRROR

Do you like what you see?

1. What color are your eyes? _____ *Blonde*

2. Would you rather have ⃝ Blue eyes ⃝ Brown eyes
   ⃝ Green eyes or ⃝ My original color rules! *Brunette*

3. What color hair do you have? _____

4. Do you wish you were a ⃝ Blonde ⃝ Brunette
   ⃝ Redhead or ⃝ Other _____?

5. Do you have ⃝ Curly hair or ⃝ Straight hair?

6. Would you rather have ⃝ Curly blond hair or
   ⃝ Straight black hair? *Long hair*

7. Is your hair ⃝ Long or ⃝ Short?

8. Would you rather have ⃝ Short hair or *Bangs*
   ⃝ Long hair?

9. ⃝ Do you like bangs or ⃝ Are they so last year?

10. ⃝ Do you wear glasses or ⃝ Do you see 20/20?

11. ⃝ Do you bite your nails or ⃝ Could you be a
    hand model? *GLASSES*

12. ⃝ Do you like wearing glasses or ⃝ Would you
    rather squint? *Brown eyes*

13. ⃝ Glasses or ⃝ Contacts?

14. Do you have ⃝ Braces or ⃝ Not? *GREEN EYES*

15. ⃝ Do you think you'll need braces or ⃝ Are you just lucky?

16. ⟡ Silver braces or ⟡ The almost invisible, clear plastic kind?

Silver

17. Would you ever wear colored contacts? ⟡ Yes! ⟡ No!

18. Are you ⟡ Too tall? ⟡ Too short? ⟡ Just right?

Tall

19. Would you rather be ⟡ Too tall or ⟡ Too Short?

Short

20. Do you consider your voice ⟡ High and squeaky? ⟡ Low and husky? or ⟡ In the middle?

Legs

21. Do you like your knees? ⟡ They're OK. ⟡ Too knobby.

22. Do you have ⟡ Long legs or ⟡ Short legs?

23. Do you think your nose is ⟡ Too big? ⟡ Too small? ⟡ Just right?

24. Do you like freckles? ⟡ They're not so bad in moderation. ⟡ Ew, get me the lemon juice!

GIRLY-GIRL

25. What's your shoe size? _____

tomboy

26. Do you like your feet? ⟡ Yes! ⟡ No or ⟡ Never thought about them!

27. Do you keep your toenails painted? ⟡ Always! or ⟡ Nope. It doesn't matter to me.

JUST RIGHT

28. Do you ⟡ Tan or ⟡ Burn?

29. Are you ⟡ A tomboy or ⟡ A girly-girl?

30. Do you prefer your clothes ⟡ Baggy or ⟡ Form-fitting?

Do you like what you see?

1. What color are your eyes? _____ *Blonde*

2. Would you rather have ⚪ Blue eyes ⚪ Brown eyes
   ⚪ Green eyes or ⚪ My original color rules! *Brunette*

3. What color hair do you have? _____

4. Do you wish you were a ⚪ Blonde ⚪ Brunette
   ⚪ Redhead or ⚪ Other _____?

5. Do you have ⚪ Curly hair or ⚪ Straight hair?

6. Would you rather have ⚪ Curly blond hair or
   ⚪ Straight black hair?   *Long hair*

7. Is your hair ⚪ Long or ⚪ Short?

8. Would you rather have ⚪ Short hair or   *Bangs*
   ⚪ Long hair?

9. ⚪ Do you like bangs or ⚪ Are they so last year?

10. ⚪ Do you wear glasses or ⚪ Do you see 20/20?

11. ⚪ Do you bite your nails or ⚪ Could you be a
    hand model?   *GLASSES*

12. ⚪ Do you like wearing glasses or ⚪ Would you
    rather squint?
                    Brown eyes

13. ⚪ Glasses or ⚪ Contacts?

14. Do you have ⚪ Braces or ⚪ Not?   *GREEN EYES*

15. ⚪ Do you think you'll need braces or ⚪ Are you just lucky?

16. ○ Silver braces or ○ The almost invisible, clear plastic kind?

    Silver

17. Would you ever wear colored contacts? ○ Yes! ○ No!

18. Are you ○ Too tall? ○ Too short? ○ Just right?

    Tall

19. Would you rather be ○ Too tall or ○ Too Short?

    Short

20. Do you consider your voice ○ High and squeaky? ○ Low and husky? or ○ In the middle?

21. Do you like your knees? ○ They're OK. ○ Too knobby.

    Legs

22. Do you have ○ Long legs or ○ Short legs?

23. Do you think your nose is ○ Too big? ○ Too small? ○ Just right?

24. Do you like freckles? ○ They're not so bad in moderation. ○ Ew, get me the lemon juice!

    GIRLY-GIRL

25. What's your shoe size? _____

    tomboy

26. Do you like your feet? ○ Yes! ○ No or ○ Never thought about them!

27. Do you keep your toenails painted? ○ Always! or ○ Nope. It doesn't matter to me.

    JUST RIGHT

28. Do you ○ Tan or ○ Burn?

29. Are you ○ A tomboy or ○ A girly-girl?

30. Do you prefer your clothes ○ Baggy or ○ Form-fitting?

Do you like what you see?

1. What color are your eyes? _____ *Blonde*

2. Would you rather have ⭕ Blue eyes ⭕ Brown eyes
   ⭕ Green eyes or ⭕ My original color rules! *Brunette*

3. What color hair do you have? _____

4. Do you wish you were a ⭕ Blonde ⭕ Brunette
   ⭕ Redhead or ⭕ Other _____?

5. Do you have ⭕ Curly hair or ⭕ Straight hair?

6. Would you rather have ⭕ Curly blond hair or
   ⭕ Straight black hair? *Long hair*

7. Is your hair ⭕ Long or ⭕ Short?

8. Would you rather have ⭕ Short hair or *Bangs*
   ⭕ Long hair?

9. ⭕ Do you like bangs or ⭕ Are they so last year?

10. ⭕ Do you wear glasses or ⭕ Do you see 20/20?

11. ⭕ Do you bite your nails or ⭕ Could you be a
    hand model? *GLASSES*

12. ⭕ Do you like wearing glasses or ⭕ Would you
    rather squint? *Brown eyes*

13. ⭕ Glasses or ⭕ Contacts? *GREEN EYES*

14. Do you have ⭕ Braces or ⭕ Not?

15. ⭕ Do you think you'll need braces or ⭕ Are you just lucky?

16. ◯ Silver braces or ◯ The almost invisible, clear plastic kind?

Silver

17. Would you ever wear colored contacts? ◯ Yes! ◯ No!

18. Are you ◯ Too tall? ◯ Too short? ◯ Just right?

Tall

19. Would you rather be ◯ Too tall or ◯ Too Short?

Short

20. Do you consider your voice ◯ High and squeaky? ◯ Low and husky? or ◯ In the middle?

Legs

21. Do you like your knees? ◯ They're OK. ◯ Too knobby.

22. Do you have ◯ Long legs or ◯ Short legs?

23. Do you think your nose is ◯ Too big? ◯ Too small? ◯ Just right?

24. Do you like freckles? ◯ They're not so bad in moderation. ◯ Ew, get me the lemon juice!

GIRLY-GIRL

25. What's your shoe size? _____

tomboy

26. Do you like your feet? ◯ Yes! ◯ No or ◯ Never thought about them!

27. Do you keep your toenails painted? ◯ Always! or ◯ Nope. It doesn't matter to me.

JUST RIGHT

28. Do you ◯ Tan or ◯ Burn?

29. Are you ◯ A tomboy or ◯ A girly-girl?

30. Do you prefer your clothes ◯ Baggy or ◯ Form-fitting?

IN YOUR CLOSET
Are you a stylista?

1. ○ Do you like to dress up or ○ Are jeans and a T-shirt as good as it gets?

2. Would you rather ○ Wear the latest style or ○ Just be comfortable?

3. ○ High heels or ○ Flats?

4. ○ Sneakers or ○ Flip-flops?

5. ○ Lots of shoes or ○ One pair for school and another for play?

6. ○ Do you wear miniskirts or ○ Do your knees never see the light of day?

7. ○ Do brand names matter or ○ Do you just wear what looks great?

8. ○ Bright colors rule or ○ All black, all the time?

9. ○ Flowered prints or ○ Stripes?

10. ○ Blue jeans or ○ Sweats?

11. Would you wear jeans with holes? ○ Absolutely!
    ○ Absolutely not!

12. ○ Sweaters or ○ Sweatshirts?

13. ○ Turtlenecks or ○ Polo shirts?

14. ○ Denim jacket or ○ Fleece jacket?

15. ○ Purse or ○ Wallet?

16. Would you rather wear ◯ A skirt and top or ◯ A dress?

17. ◯ Straight fitted skirt or ◯ Long flowing skirt?

18. ◯ Do you like to coordinate or ◯ Do you just pull out whatever's clean?

19. ◯ Bikini or ◯ One-piece?

20. Would you rather get a gift certificate for ◯ A clothing store or ◯ A bookstore?

21. ◯ Do you like to shop or ◯ Would you rather have 1,000 needles stuck in your eye?

22. Do you think you have style? ◯ Yes ◯ No or ◯ Maybe

23. Who is the most stylish of all your friends? _____

24. What public figure would you most want to dress like?

_____

25. Can you sew? ◯ Yes ◯ No

26. Do you like to sew? ◯ Yes ◯ Not even if my life depended on it!

27. ◯ Knit ◯ Crochet or ◯ Neither?

28. If neither, do you want to learn? ◯ Absolutely!
◯ Absolutely NOT!

29. Do you ◯ Change your fingernail color to match your clothes? ◯ Keep one color or ◯ No polish at all?

30. ◯ Do you change what you wear by the season or
◯ Do you wear shorts in the winter?

IN YOUR CLOSET
Are you a stylista?

1. ○ Do you like to dress up or ○ Are jeans and a T-shirt as good as it gets?

2. Would you rather ○ Wear the latest style or ○ Just be comfortable?

3. ○ High heels or ○ Flats?

4. ○ Sneakers or ○ Flip-flops?

5. ○ Lots of shoes or ○ One pair for school and another for play?

6. ○ Do you wear miniskirts or ○ Do your knees never see the light of day?

7. ○ Do brand names matter or ○ Do you just wear what looks great?

8. ○ Bright colors rule or ○ All black, all the time?

9. ○ Flowered prints or ○ Stripes?

10. ○ Blue jeans or ○ Sweats?

11. Would you wear jeans with holes? ○ Absolutely! ○ Absolutely not!

12. ○ Sweaters or ○ Sweatshirts?

13. ○ Turtlenecks or ○ Polo shirts?

14. ○ Denim jacket or ○ Fleece jacket?

15. ○ Purse or ○ Wallet?

16. Would you rather wear ○ A skirt and top or ○ A dress?

17. ○ Straight fitted skirt or ○ Long flowing skirt?

18. ○ Do you like to coordinate or ○ Do you just pull out whatever's clean?

19. ○ Bikini or ○ One-piece?

20. Would you rather get a gift certificate for
○ A clothing store or ○ A bookstore?

21. ○ Do you like to shop or ○ Would you rather have 1,000 needles stuck in your eye?

22. Do you think you have style? ○ Yes ○ No or ○ Maybe

23. Who is the most stylish of all your friends? _____

24. What public figure would you most want to dress like?

_____

25. Can you sew? ○ Yes ○ No

26. Do you like to sew? ○ Yes ○ Not even if my life depended on it!

27. ○ Knit ○ Crochet or ○ Neither?

28. If neither, do you want to learn? ○ Absolutely!
○ Absolutely NOT!

29. Do you ○ Change your fingernail color to match your clothes? ○ Keep one color or ○ No polish at all?

30. ○ Do you change what you wear by the season or
○ Do you wear shorts in the winter?

IN YOUR CLOSET
are you a stylista?

1. ○ Do you like to dress up or ○ Are jeans and a T-shirt as good as it gets?

2. Would you rather ○ Wear the latest style or ○ Just be comfortable?

3. ○ High heels or ○ Flats?

4. ○ Sneakers or ○ Flip-flops?

5. ○ Lots of shoes or ○ One pair for school and another for play?

6. ○ Do you wear miniskirts or ○ Do your knees never see the light of day?

7. ○ Do brand names matter or ○ Do you just wear what looks great?

8. ○ Bright colors rule or ○ All black, all the time?

9. ○ Flowered prints or ○ Stripes?

10. ○ Blue jeans or ○ Sweats?

11. Would you wear jeans with holes? ○ Absolutely!
○ Absolutely not!

12. ○ Sweaters or ○ Sweatshirts?

13. ○ Turtlenecks or ○ Polo shirts?

14. ○ Denim jacket or ○ Fleece jacket?

15. ○ Purse or ○ Wallet?

16. Would you rather wear ⭕ A skirt and top or ⭕ A dress?

17. ⭕ Straight fitted skirt or ⭕ Long flowing skirt?

18. ⭕ Do you like to coordinate or ⭕ Do you just pull out whatever's clean?

19. ⭕ Bikini or ⭕ One-piece?

20. Would you rather get a gift certificate for ⭕ A clothing store or ⭕ A bookstore?

21. ⭕ Do you like to shop or ⭕ Would you rather have 1,000 needles stuck in your eye?

22. Do you think you have style? ⭕ Yes ⭕ No or ⭕ Maybe

23. Who is the most stylish of all your friends? _____

24. What public figure would you most want to dress like?

_____

25. Can you sew? ⭕ Yes ⭕ No

26. Do you like to sew? ⭕ Yes ⭕ Not even if my life depended on it!

27. ⭕ Knit ⭕ Crochet or ⭕ Neither?

28. If neither, do you want to learn? ⭕ Absolutely!
⭕ Absolutely NOT!

29. Do you ⭕ Change your fingernail color to match your clothes? ⭕ Keep one color or ⭕ No polish at all?

30. ⭕ Do you change what you wear by the season or
⭕ Do you wear shorts in the winter?

IN YOUR CLOSET
Are you a stylista?

1. ◯ Do you like to dress up or ◯ Are jeans and a T-shirt as good as it gets?

2. Would you rather ◯ Wear the latest style or ◯ Just be comfortable?

3. ◯ High heels or ◯ Flats?

4. ◯ Sneakers or ◯ Flip-flops?

5. ◯ Lots of shoes or ◯ One pair for school and another for play?

6. ◯ Do you wear miniskirts or ◯ Do your knees never see the light of day?

7. ◯ Do brand names matter or ◯ Do you just wear what looks great?

8. ◯ Bright colors rule or ◯ All black, all the time?

9. ◯ Flowered prints or ◯ Stripes?

10. ◯ Blue jeans or ◯ Sweats?

11. Would you wear jeans with holes? ◯ Absolutely! ◯ Absolutely not!

12. ◯ Sweaters or ◯ Sweatshirts?

13. ◯ Turtlenecks or ◯ Polo shirts?

14. ◯ Denim jacket or ◯ Fleece jacket?

15. ◯ Purse or ◯ Wallet?

16. Would you rather wear ◯ A skirt and top or ◯ A dress?

17. ◯ Straight fitted skirt or ◯ Long flowing skirt?

18. ◯ Do you like to coordinate or ◯ Do you just pull out whatever's clean?

19. ◯ Bikini or ◯ One-piece?

20. Would you rather get a gift certificate for
◯ A clothing store or ◯ A bookstore?

21. ◯ Do you like to shop or ◯ Would you rather have 1,000 needles stuck in your eye?

22. Do you think you have style? ◯ Yes ◯ No or ◯ Maybe

23. Who is the most stylish of all your friends? _____

24. What public figure would you most want to dress like?

_____

25. Can you sew? ◯ Yes ◯ No

26. Do you like to sew? ◯ Yes ◯ Not even if my life depended on it!

27. ◯ Knit ◯ Crochet or ◯ Neither?

28. If neither, do you want to learn? ◯ Absolutely!
◯ Absolutely NOT!

29. Do you ◯ Change your fingernail color to match your clothes? ◯ Keep one color or ◯ No polish at all?

30. ◯ Do you change what you wear by the season or
◯ Do you wear shorts in the winter?

FOR YOU AND YOUR BEST FRIEND ONLY

Nobody knows you like your best friend—or does she? Answer the questions like you think your best friend would. Have her do the same for you.

Then swap!

1. Favorite color? _____

2. Favorite fast food? _____

3. Middle name? _____

4. ⬜ Dark chocolate or ⬜ Milk chocolate?

5. ⬜ Chai tea latte or ⬜ Peppermint mocha cappuccino?

6. Favorite holiday? _____

7. ⬜ Cat person or ⬜ Dog person?

8. Pet's name? _____

9. Favorite school subject? _____

10. Secret crush? _____

11. ⬜ Shy or ⬜ Social butterfly?

12. Favorite game? _____

13. Favorite book? _____

14. Pet peeves? _____

15. Eye color? _____

16. Hated vegetable? _____

17. Favorite famous person? _____

18. Favorite musician? _____

19. Sports: ○ Play or ○ Watch?

20. Favorite cafeteria food? _____

21. What won't she eat in the cafeteria? _____

22. ○ Orange or ○ Apple?

23. Favorite teacher? _____

24. ○ Summer ○ Winter ○ Spring or ○ Fall?

25. ○ Skiing or ○ Swimming?

26. ○ Potato chips or ○ Pretzels?

27. Room color? _____

28. Roller coasters: ○ Bring it on! ○ Stay on the ground, thank you!

29. Must have: ○ Cell phone or ○ MP3 player?

30. Birthday? _____

FOR YOU AND YOUR BEST FRIEND ONLY

Nobody knows you like your best friend—or does she? Answer the questions like you think your best friend would. Have her do the same for you.

Then swap!

1. Favorite color? _____

2. Favorite fast food? _____

3. Middle name? _____

4. ◯ Dark chocolate or ◯ Milk chocolate?

5. ◯ Chai tea latte or ◯ Peppermint mocha cappuccino?

6. Favorite holiday? _____

7. ◯ Cat person or ◯ Dog person?

8. Pet's name? _____

9. Favorite school subject? _____

10. Secret crush? _____

11. ◯ Shy or ◯ Social butterfly?

12. Favorite game? _____

13. Favorite book? _____

14. Pet peeves? _____

15. Eye color? _____

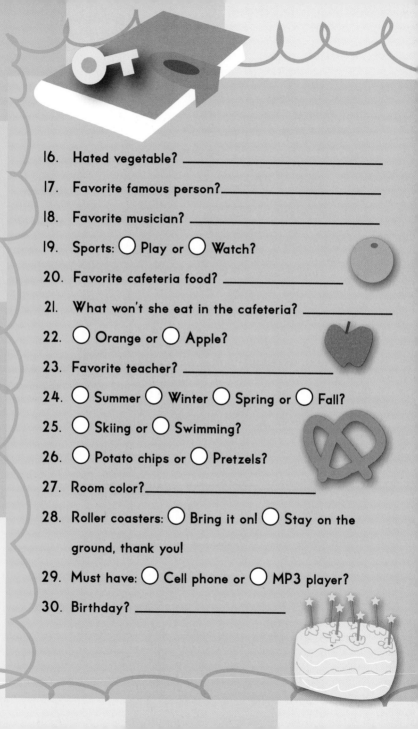

16. Hated vegetable? _____

17. Favorite famous person? _____

18. Favorite musician? _____

19. Sports: ⃝ Play or ⃝ Watch?

20. Favorite cafeteria food? _____

21. What won't she eat in the cafeteria? _____

22. ⃝ Orange or ⃝ Apple?

23. Favorite teacher? _____

24. ⃝ Summer ⃝ Winter ⃝ Spring or ⃝ Fall?

25. ⃝ Skiing or ⃝ Swimming?

26. ⃝ Potato chips or ⃝ Pretzels?

27. Room color? _____

28. Roller coasters: ⃝ Bring it on! ⃝ Stay on the ground, thank you!

29. Must have: ⃝ Cell phone or ⃝ MP3 player?

30. Birthday? _____